Dragon Boat Festival

Traditional Chinese Festival

It is the

Dragon Boat Festival.

We went to see the

Dragon Boat races.

We made **rice dumplings** to take to the races.

5

We saw the boats.

The boats were very,
very long.

This is the drummer.
She played the drum,
when the boat
was racing.

The boats went faster and faster and faster.

Splash... splash... splash!

This is the **flag catcher**. He got the flag at the end of the race.

13

We had fun at the Dragon Boat races.

Glossary

 flag catcher

 rice dumplings